D1441897

HELPLINE
TEEN ISSUES AND ANSWERS ™

RAPE AND SEXUAL ASSAULT
HEALING AND RECOVERY

REBECCA T. KLEIN

ROSEN
PUBLISHING®

New York

Published in 2014 by The Rosen Publishing Group, Inc.
29 East 21st Street, New York, NY 10010

Library of Congress Cataloging-in-Publication Data

Klein, Rebecca T.
Rape and sexual assault: healing and recovery/Rebecca T. Klein.—First edition.
    pages cm.—(Helpline: teen issues and answers)
Includes bibliographical references and index.
ISBN 978-1-4488-9449-9 (library binding)
1. Rape victims. 2. Rape victims—Rehabilitation 3. Sexually abused teenagers.
4. Sexually abused teenagers—Rehabilitation. I. Title.
HV6558.K556 2013
362.883—dc23

                                                                2012041016

Manufactured in the United States of America

CPSIA Compliance Information: Batch #S13YA: For further information, contact Rosen Publishing, New York, New York, at 1-800-237-9932.

CONTENTS

Maybe you're reading this because you have a friend who has been sexually assaulted and you are trying to understand her experience. Maybe you are doing research for a paper or simply seeking knowledge for knowledge's sake. Whatever your reason for reading, and especially if you are a survivor or a friend of a survivor, it is important to remember that there is no panacea for recovering from a sexual assault or rape. It is an ongoing process, and no one moves through that process in exactly the same way. Here, you will find an overview of many issues that are common to lots of survivors of sexual assault, but there is no way to be sure that everything a survivor might experience is covered. The advice given here is based on research and conversation, but you are encouraged to seek out other resources as well. Visit the Web sites of the organizations mentioned throughout, and check out the books mentioned in the For Further Reading section. Keep in mind that everyone's experience is unique, and so is their recovery. This is why self-care is so important and why finding a professional counselor or therapist with whom you connect can be so helpful. A therapist can work with you to develop a plan for your specific recovery.

We will begin by discussing the different types of sexual assault and rape. Often, the recovery process is hindered by the fact that the victim does not recognize the experience as assault, which is one

If you are dealing with rape or any other type of sexual assault, it can be incredibly helpful to have someone you can talk to.

reason why it's important to cover these definitions. The second section covers the processes of visiting the emergency room and reporting the crime immediately after the assault. The third discusses some of the common effects of sexual assault, while the fourth and fifth sections offer advice on healing and taking back power through supporting others and helping others to heal. This structure is meant to mirror the process of recovery, of first under-standing and naming what has happened to you, then dealing with the immediate effects, and eventually moving from feeling like a victim to feeling like a survivor. After reading the information contained here, continue to seek out other sources of advice and support, whether you are a survivor, a loved one of a survivor, or someone who is simply seeking to understand the process of recovering from rape and sexual assault. The more we learn about sexual violence, its effects, and how to help people recover, the more we can do to help each other heal.

Defining Rape and Sexual Assault

When you have experienced a trauma like rape or sexual assault, it is incredibly important and helpful to be able to give words to the experience, to name it so that you can begin to recover. When something horrible happens and you don't know how to describe it, it can be very hard to talk to others about it, or even to process it in your own mind. Giving a name to the horrible thing that happened can help pin it down so that you can begin to process it, deal with it, and recover from it. Rape and sexual assault take many forms, and people use lots of different terms to talk about these forms. All that language can be confusing, and it helps to have a breakdown of all the various words. Let's talk about those terms and what they mean.

After experiencing a rape or assault, it can be hard to organize all of the thoughts in your head. Sometimes, knowing the common terminology for your experience can help.

SEXUAL ASSAULT

An assault is any type of attack by a person upon another person, using verbal or physical force. Sexual assault happens when someone is attacked without consent in a

I Don't Know If It Was Assault...

If something traumatic has happened to you but it does not fit any of these descriptions, do not by any means feel that you need to discount your experience. Some sexual experiences are very much in a gray area. For instance, if you didn't say no or physically resist, but you still felt coerced or pressured, it can be hard to make sense of the situation. But remember, just because something does not fit a legal definition of rape or assault does not mean that it hasn't affected the person to whom it happened. Any sort of sexual experience that leaves you feeling upset, taken advantage of, manipulated, or dehumanized deserves processing and attention. Even if there are not legal steps to take in the situation, therapy can help, and many of the same recovery techniques used by survivors of rape and sexual assault can be useful. If you are struggling with any kind of sexual experience that has negatively affected you, consider speaking with a school counselor, a parent, or another adult that you trust about what happened. That person can direct you toward resources to help you deal with your experience, and sometimes just speaking to someone else about what happened and how you feel can be a huge step toward recovery.

sexual manner. The word "rape" is used when the attack involves sexual intercourse. Sexual intercourse means penetration—that is, when someone puts something inside your body, whether it is a penis, fingers, or a foreign object. We will discuss rape in more detail later in this section, and we'll talk about the different types of rape that can occur. It is also important to know, however, that

You should seek guidance and support any time you are dealing with a sexual experience that made you feel uncomfortable, even if you don't think it was technically an assault.

rape is not the only form of sexual assault. Any sexual behavior that occurs without consent is considered assault. Here are a few other forms of sexual assault.

GROPING

Groping happens whenever someone touches any part of a person's body in a way that person doesn't welcome. Groping can occur over or under the clothes, and it can happen behind closed doors or in public. If you are walking up the stairs and someone grabs your butt from behind, that's groping. If you are sitting with someone alone in a classroom or in a crowded movie theater, and that person puts a hand up your shirt without your consent, that's groping. When someone puts a hand on or near your crotch without consent, that's definitely groping. Even touches on the arm or leg can take on characteristics of groping, depending on the nature of the touch. Remember that your body is your body, and you have the right to refuse any unwanted touch. If someone touches you in a way that makes you feel uncomfortable, tell that person in no uncertain terms to stop. If he or she does not stop when you say so, report the person to an adult that you trust. Groping is a form of sexual assault. You do not have to put up with it, and anyone who is doing it should not get away with it.

SEXUAL HARASSMENT

Sexual assault is not limited to physical acts. Harassment is a form of assault, too, although many victims do not recognize their experience as harassment. Sexual harassment includes lewd comments, indecent exposure, and other coercive sexual acts that may not be physical but can still be traumatic. When someone forces another person to look at pictures depicting nudity or sexual acts, it is harassment. If a student spreads sexual rumors about a classmate or calls that classmate names that have sexual connotations, it can qualify as harassment. Certainly, if a teacher, a coach, or any other authority figure says things or shows things of a sexual nature to a young person, whether those things are directly related to the young person or not, it is harassment. Sometimes, an authority figure will use the power of his or her position to intimidate young people into staying silent about harassment. Don't let that prevent you from speaking out. If you feel like you are being sexually harassed, tell an adult immediately. You do not have to deal with behavior that makes you feel violated, scared, or uncomfortable, even if nothing physical has occurred.

CHILD SEXUAL ABUSE

Child sexual abuse occurs when an adult or an older teenager engages in sexual acts with a child. Like all sexual assault, child sexual abuse includes but is not limited to rape. Often, child sexual abuse is ongoing and is perpetrated by an adult that the child should be able to trust, such as a family member, a family friend, or a teacher. Because of its ongoing nature and the extreme violation of trust that accompanies it, child sexual abuse can have long-lasting

A school counselor or a therapist can be instrumental in helping you deal with your assault. These professionals have many techniques and tools at their disposal to help you recover.

and extremely traumatic effects on a person's emotional development. This is often compounded by the fact that family members may deny that the abuse happened or encourage the victim to stay silent. If you are being abused, or if you have been abused in the past, you do not have to carry that burden around alone. If family members are not supportive, talk to a school counselor or another adult. If there are no adults in your life that you trust, find the number of an abuse hotline. There are many resources available to help you begin to heal.

RAPE

As we mentioned, rape is sexual assault that includes penetration. Often, people think of rape as being limited to a man putting his penis inside a woman's vagina or anus, but that is not the only form of rape. Rape includes penetration with the fingers or with foreign objects, and men can be raped, too. Anytime someone puts something inside another person's body without his or her consent, that's rape. Forced oral sex, while it may be legally defined as sexual assault, rather than rape, is generally included. There are many different types of rape. Often, people who are raped do not report the crime because they don't think that they were truly raped. For instance, some people think that if the rapist was a significant other or spouse, the rape doesn't qualify as a crime. Others think that if they did not fight back, did not struggle physically against their attacker, that it wasn't rape. That is absolutely untrue. Anytime someone has sexual intercourse with another person without consent, no matter who the person is, it qualifies as rape. If the victim is unconscious or in any other way unable to give consent, it also qualifies as rape. People give different names to different types of rape, generally based on the attacker's relationship to the victim. But no matter how these types are categorized, remember that no form of rape is more valid than any other; they are all equal violations. The bottom line is, sexual intercourse without consent is rape, and it is illegal. Period.

A large percentage of rapes are "acquaintance rapes," meaning that the rape is committed by someone who is known to the person who is assaulted.

TYPES OF RAPE

Stranger rape is what first comes to mind when most people think of rape. This is rape in which the attacker is completely unknown to the victim. It could occur in the street, in the home as part of a home invasion, or any number of other places. It is often difficult to identify the attacker in these types of situations. The attacker may wear something to obscure his appearance, or he may blindfold the victim or otherwise hinder the victim's vision.

Also, it can be more difficult to identify someone you've seen only once, in a traumatic situation where your memory may be affected. This makes it very important to report the crime as soon as possible so that evidence can be gathered.

Incestuous rape is rape that is committed by a family member. This type of rape often goes unreported because, like all forms of child sexual abuse, it is stigmatized by society and often covered up or denied by the family members who know about it. Victims often fear the consequences of reporting incestuous rape. They are afraid of being judged, of not being believed, and of tearing their families apart. According to the Rape, Abuse, and Incest National Network (RAINN), 7 percent of all rapes are committed by a family member.

Acquaintance rape refers to rape by someone with whom the victim is familiar. The attacker could be a friend, a coach, a teacher, or a friend of the family. Acquaintance rape is the most common type of rape. It includes date rape. According to the National Center for Victims of Crime, 77 percent of rapes are committed by attackers who are known to their victims. This means that acquaintance rape is far more common than stranger rape.

Incestuous rape, date rape, and other forms of acquaintance rape and sexual assault often go unreported. There are lots of reasons for this, including fear and lack of knowledge about the reporting process. Next, we will discuss some of the fears people face when deciding whether or not to report their assault, and we will talk about the benefits of overcoming those fears and reporting the attack.

MYTH Only women can be sexually assaulted, and only men can be the perpetrators.

FACT This is absolutely untrue. There are many, many male abuse/assault victims, and there are female perpetrators. Statistics from the Centers for Disease Control and Prevention (CDC) indicate that 4.2 percent of boys in grades nine through twelve reported having been raped at some point in their lives. This figure does not account for other types of sexual assault. If you are a boy and have been raped or assaulted, do not feel ashamed or alone. Tell someone what has happened and seek help. Whether you are a girl or a boy, do not think that a woman has any more right to touch you against your will than a man does. Unwanted sexual contact is wrong, period, regardless of the gender of the abuser or the victim.

MYTH Being sexually assaulted by someone of the same sex makes you gay.

FACT This is completely false. If you are heterosexual, nothing will "turn you gay," including abuse. If you are homosexual or bisexual, nothing will "turn you straight." Sexual assault has nothing to do with your sexual orientation. Being forced into a sexual act does not indicate anything about your preferences or anything at all about you. It is entirely the fault of your attacker; it is entirely about your attacker. That brings us to the next myth.

MYTH Sexual assault is about sex.

FACT In reality, sexual assault has very little to do with sex. It is about power and control. The attacker, possibly due to feeling powerless in other areas of his or her life, attempts to exert control over another person. Sex is the weapon the attacker uses to exert this control, but the assault is not really about sex. This is why it is so ridiculous to say that a victim "brought it on herself" by dressing sexily or behaving in a provocative manner. A person who will rape or assault another person will do it no matter what the victim is wearing or how he or she is behaving because the act is not about sex at all.

CHAPTER 2

Visiting the Emergency Room and Reporting the Crime

Recovering from rape or sexual assault is a long process, and people move through it in different ways. It may take longer for some people than for others, and the steps of recovery may not be the same for each person. For everyone, however, recovery begins by dealing with the immediate aftermath of the assault. It can be incredibly difficult to think rationally after an assault. As much as you may just want to forget the entire incident, professional help is essential to make sure that you are OK and to begin the recovery process. Ideally, you should find an adult that you trust and tell that person about the incident so that he or she can guide you to the resources you need. However, if you can't bring yourself to talk to an adult, at least talk to a friend that you trust. It's very important that you have some help in dealing with

In the immediate aftermath of an assault, it is helpful to have a professional advocate or an adult that you trust to help you deal with the medical and legal steps you need to follow.

the immediate steps, since you may be too traumatized to think clearly.

There are two extremely important types of attention that a victim of rape or assault should consider seeking as soon as possible: medical attention and legal attention. Although everyone should move through the recovery process at their own pace, there are several reasons to seek medical and legal attention as soon as possible after being raped or assaulted. Doing so can protect your health and increase the chances of bringing your attacker to justice. We will discuss why it is so important to seek immediate legal and medical attention. We'll also discuss what happens in the emergency room and what happens during the process of reporting the attack to the police.

SEEKING MEDICAL ATTENTION

After removing yourself from immediate danger, seeking medical attention is the very first thing you should do after being sexually assaulted. You should go to the hospital even before you contact the police; you can call the police from the emergency room, or have someone call them for you. Lots of people find it very helpful to have someone they trust go through the reporting process with them from the beginning and be present in the emergency room. If you have a family member with whom you are especially close, you may want to ask him or her to do this. However, many people find that it is easier to call a friend instead of a family member. Either way, there is no reason to feel weird about asking someone to come with you. The medical part of the reporting process can feel very invasive, and it is absolutely understandable to need someone you trust to be there with you while it happens.

For a lot of people who have been raped or assaulted, seeking medical attention is the hardest step because it requires admitting out loud, immediately, what has happened. Although it is difficult and you may want to shower or just be alone and hide from the world, it is very

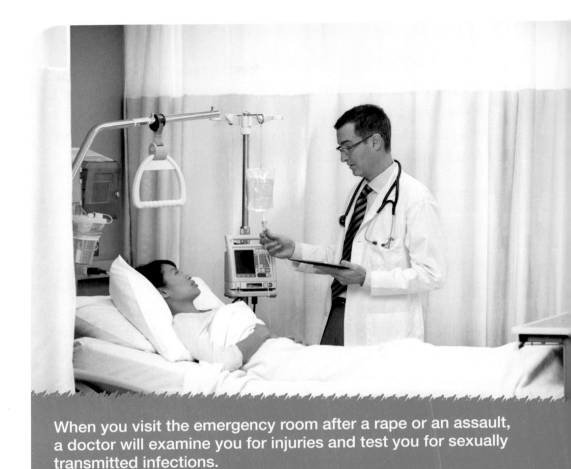

When you visit the emergency room after a rape or an assault, a doctor will examine you for injuries and test you for sexually transmitted infections.

important to see a doctor first. There are several reasons why medical attention is time-sensitive in the case of rape or sexual assault. For one thing, any injuries you've sustained need to be examined and treated as quickly as possible. A doctor can look at any bruises or fractures and can assess whether you have any internal injuries or other physical effects from the assault. The doctor can also take measures to decrease the chances of pregnancy or of contracting a sexually transmitted infection (STI) from the assault. These measures are more effective if you see the doctor immediately, the sooner the better. Also, if you visit the emergency room before you shower, the medical staff may be able to collect evidence that could help police find and/or arrest your attacker.

WHAT WILL HAPPEN IN THE EMERGENCY ROOM?

It may be reassuring to know the specific steps that medical professionals will take when you come to the emergency room after being sexually assaulted. First, the doctor will check for any obvious injuries such as fractures, cuts, or bruises. Then he or she will collect evidence. (This evidence is usually referred to as a rape kit. There is more detailed information about rape kits in the next section.) After collecting evidence, the doctor will run a blood test. If you are female, you will be tested to see if you are pregnant. The doctor can also give you Plan B, which is often called the "morning-after pill," to prevent pregnancy. According to the American Academy of Family Physicians (AAFP), this treatment can reduce your chances of becoming pregnant by 60 to 90 percent.

Whether you are male or female, you will be tested for STIs. The AAFP says that 5 to 10 percent of rape victims contract an STI. The doctor who treats you can prescribe medication for syphilis, gonorrhea, and chlamydia, and he or she will tell you about medicines that can help prevent

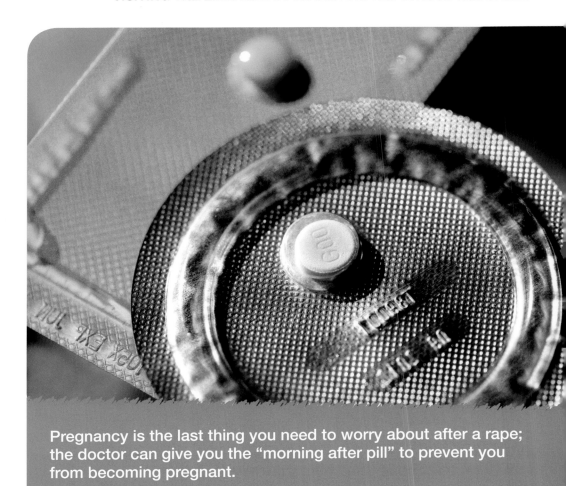

Pregnancy is the last thing you need to worry about after a rape; the doctor can give you the "morning after pill" to prevent you from becoming pregnant.

you from contracting HIV (although, again according to the AAFP, the chance of getting HIV from rape is less than 1 percent). It is also a good idea to get vaccinated for hepatitis B, if you haven't already had the vaccination. The doctor will give you the first dose immediately, and then you will need follow-up doses in one month and in six months.

Health care professionals are required to call the police if they are aware of sexual assault or abuse, or even if they suspect it. However, the hospital's obligation to call does not mean that the patient is obligated to talk to the police when they arrive. The decision to cooperate with the police is entirely up to the patient. But there are many good reasons to do so, reasons that will be covered later on in this section.

WHAT IS A RAPE KIT?

To collect evidence in the emergency room after a rape, doctors usually use what is referred to as a rape kit. Using magnifying glasses, plastic baggies, and microscope slides, the doctor will collect any semen, saliva, hairs, or fibers that the attacker may have left on your body. All of these things can help in identifying the attacker and bringing him to justice. The saliva, semen, and hair all contain the attacker's DNA, which is a unique genetic code that belongs only to the attacker. If your attacker is already in the legal system for a previous crime, DNA evidence can identify him and match him to your rape. If your rapist is caught afterward, his DNA can be tested and compared with the DNA found in your rape kit. Police can use a rape kit to immediately pursue your attacker. Even if you are hesitant about cooperating with a police investigation, you should still have a rape kit done. It can be essential in getting your attacker off the street.

SEXUAL ASSAULT EVIDENCE COLLECTION KIT
CAT. NO. VEC100

MEDICAL PERSONNEL
PLEASE PRINT

VICTIM'S NAME: _____
CASE NUMBER: _____
ATTENDING PHYSICAN/NURSE: _____
HOSPITAL/CLINIC: _____
KIT SEALED BY: _____

AFFIX
BIOHAZARD
SEAL HERE

PLACE SEALED KIT AND CLOTHING BAGS IN SECURE AND REFRIGERATED STORAGE
AREA AFTER EVIDENCE COLLECTION

PLACED BY: _____
DATE: _____
TIME: _____ am pm

POLICE PERSONNEL
CHAIN OF POSSESSION

RECEIVED FROM: _____
DATE: _____ TIME: _____ am pm
RECEIVED FROM: _____
DATE: _____ TIME: _____ am pm
RECEIVED FROM: _____
DATE: _____ TIME: _____ am pm
RECEIVED FROM: _____
DATE: _____ TIME: _____ am pm

DELIVER SEALED KIT AND CLOTHING BAGS TO THE CRIME LABORATORY IMMEDIATELY

FORENSIC LABORATORY PERSONNEL

LABORATORY NUMBER: _____
POLICE CASE NUMBER: _____

MANUFACTURED BY SIRCHIE® FINGER PRINT LABORATORIES, INC.
100 HUNTER PLACE, YOUNGSVILLE, N.C. 27596 U.S.A.
PHONE: (919) 554-2244, (800) 356-7311• FAX: (919) 554-2266, (800) 899-8181

SEXUAL ASSAULT EVIDENCE COLLECTION KIT
SIRCHIE

REORDER NO.: VEC100

In the emergency room, medical professionals will collect evidence for a rape kit. This evidence can be essential in helping police bring your attacker to justice.

SEEKING LEGAL ATTENTION

The process of seeking legal attention begins in the emergency room when medical professionals run the rape kit. After medical treatment, you can call 911, have a friend or family member call for you, or let the hospital staff make the call, as they are required to do so if no one else does. You have a choice of whether or not to cooperate with the police and answer their questions. You are not legally obligated to do so. However, there are many reasons why cooperating is helpful to you and to others. Seeking justice by giving the police information about your attacker can help you regain your sense of control. It also increases the chances of catching your attacker and getting him off the street, therefore preventing him from assaulting more people. Your first priority, of course, should be to take care of yourself. But if you are at all able to handle the process of reporting, you should do it. Again, reporting the crime can help you feel that you are taking back some of the control that was taken from you during the assault. Even if you do not report the attack immediately, legal action can be taken months after the assault. However, as we discussed, the sooner you report it, the better the chances of catching the attacker. It is a good idea to have a police report on file right away. You may need some time to decide whether you want to pursue prosecution and go through a trial. But if you report the rape immediately, the evidence and police report will be there when and if you decide to pursue the case.

Reporting Ongoing Abuse

If you are in a situation where you have been repeatedly raped or assaulted over a long period of time by a family member or another person in your life, the process of recognizing and reporting the crime is not going to be as straightforward as it is in the case of a single incident. Of course, if you visit the emergency room right after being raped, the evidence can be collected in the same way. But if you know that you are being abused or assaulted, or have been in the past, you should definitely not wait to report. Immediately talk with someone who can help you get out of the situation and get to a safe place. If the first person you talk to dismisses you or doesn't believe you, talk to someone else. Call the number of one of the organizations in the For More Information section. If you don't feel comfortable talking to an adult, talk to a friend. You may find that it is easier to approach an adult with a friend by your side supporting you.

If you are not being abused but you suspect that one of your friends may be, try to get him or her to talk to you. Kids who are being sexually abused often become depressed and emotionally withdrawn, and they are unusually secretive about their home lives. They may also be unusually interested in sex, having more knowledge about it than other kids their age, or they may completely avoid the subject altogether. If you feel that something isn't right with a friend and you are worried, try to get him or her to open up. Don't push your friend or make assumptions, but make it clear that you are there to listen without judgment. Having someone to trust and talk to is absolutely essential in reporting and stopping ongoing sexual abuse.

WHAT HAPPENS WHEN I REPORT?

Generally, after you call (or have someone else call) to report the attack, the police will come to you to do the interview and take your statement. If you have gone to the hospital, this will likely happen there. It is a good idea to have the details of the incident straight in your mind before speaking with the police. Writing everything down can be a great help in organizing your thoughts. Also, if you have the details written, you can refer to your notes during the interview if you get flustered. Even if you choose not to write things down, it will help to go over the incident verbally with someone else before you speak with the police.

When you report a rape or assault, the police will ask you a lot of questions about the details of the incident, and some of them may feel intrusive or make you feel uncomfortable. You shouldn't let this deter you from reporting, but you should prepare yourself mentally for the interview. You will be required to discuss the details of the attack, and you may need to answer these questions many times over in different ways. This does not mean that the officer thinks you are lying; he or she is just trying to gather detailed evidence to build the strongest case possible against your attacker.

The police may also collect physical evidence that was not collected during the examination in the emergency room. They may want to visit the scene of the attack to see if any fluids or fibers have been left behind. They will look for any physical details that might help identify the attacker.

If you need more advice about reporting, need someone to advocate for you, or just need moral support during the reporting process, call your local rape crisis center. It can provide you with a trained volunteer who can help you through the process and may even accompany you to the interview. RAINN can connect you with a local center through its hotline, 1-800-656-HOPE (4673).

CHAPTER 3

Physical and Psychological Effects of Sexual Assault

Another important aspect of recovery is to learn about the effects that a rape or assault can have physically, emotionally, and psychologically. It is difficult to deal with an emotion or even a physical symptom when you're not sure exactly what is happening. Being able to name the symptom can be the first step in overcoming it. When you know what you're dealing with, you are better able to look for resources that can help you cope. It also makes it easier to explain your symptoms to other people who may be able to help you and guide you to the resources you need.

No two people will react to sexual assault in the exact same way, and everyone's recovery process will be different. The nature of the effects, especially the psychological ones, may vary based on factors such as the age of the victim and the type of attack. For instance, someone who is attacked by a stranger will probably experience different emotions and reactions than someone who is abused over a long period of time by a family member or authority figure. All types of assault are traumatic in different ways. But there are some symptoms that are very common to many survivors of rape and sexual assault. We will discuss those symptoms in this section.

PHYSICAL EFFECTS

There are several physical symptoms that can result from rape or sexual assault. As we discussed earlier, this is one of the reasons why it is so important to seek a doctor's care as soon as possible after an attack. Immediate care will minimize the long-term effects of many physical symptoms and help make you healthy so that you can begin your emotional recovery.

Penetration, whether with a penis, fingers, or other foreign objects, can cause bleeding or tearing of the vaginal or anal tissue. This is very common in rapes and assaults, since the penetration occurs against the victim's will and therefore the body is not prepared for it. This is painful and, if the bleeding or tearing it is not treated quickly, can cause infection. This is one of the symptoms that should be treated right away by a doctor.

Sexual intercourse of any kind, including rape, can cause a urinary tract infection (UTI). UTIs occur when bacteria found around the anus gets into the urethra, which happens a lot during sex and can definitely happen

The physical effects of a sexual assault can add to the trauma, but they are much more manageable if you seek a doctor's care and advice.

in a sexual assault. They can make you feel very uncomfortable. If untreated, a UTI can turn into a bladder infection, which is even more uncomfortable and dangerous. A doctor can test for and treat a UTI following a sexual assault. The treatment will decrease discomfort and prevent the infection from spreading.

To reiterate what was said in the last section on emergency care, you should also have a doctor test you for STIs following any type of sexual assault. In some cases, doctors may be able to give you medicine to prevent an infection from taking hold. Even if they are not able to prevent the infection, the sooner you begin treatment, the sooner your body can heal.

Another big reason to seek immediate medical attention after a rape is to prevent pregnancy. If you are on any form of birth control, your chances of becoming pregnant are very slim, though you should still be tested. If you are not on any form of contraception, it is even more essential. Pregnancy after a rape brings on all sorts of other questions and issues that you do not need to deal with in addition to coping with the attack itself. The doctor can take measures to make sure that you don't become pregnant and, therefore, don't have to confront those issues.

When you deal with the physical aspects of sexual assault right away, your body can begin to heal itself and return to a more normal state. Physical wellness and comfort are incredibly important when dealing with the emotional and psychological effects of assault. The quicker your body heals, the more energy you will have to put toward healing your mind.

PSYCHOLOGICAL EFFECTS

Once you've sought treatment for the physical effects of sexual assault, you can begin to deal with the way it impacts your mind. Often, this part is much more difficult.

You may be so traumatized from the attack that you cannot think clearly. Sorting out your emotions and thought processes may be more than you can handle, which is why it helps to talk with a counselor or therapist. Again, each person is different, and no two people react to assault in the same way. There is no one prescribed recovery process and no "wrong" way to react or cope. But there are symptoms that a lot of people experience after a rape or sexual assault.

SELF-BLAME

Many victims go through a thought process in which they blame themselves for the attack, rationalizing ways they could have prevented it from happening. They think that if they had dressed differently or behaved differently, they would not have been assaulted. This is a harmful thought process. Rape, or any other type of assault, is 100 percent the fault of the attacker and 0 percent the fault of the victim. In some ways, blaming yourself is an attempt to take control of the situation. But directing blame or anger toward yourself can become toxic and hinder your recovery. Put the blame

It is very common for victims of rape and sexual assault to try to shoulder some of the blame for the attack. Even if you feel this way, remember that the fault lies with your attacker.

where it belongs—on your attacker—and take control by focusing on healing yourself as completely as possible.

Another aspect of self-blame, which is sometimes very hard to talk about, is the fact that occasionally, the victim will feel some sort of physical pleasure from the assault. This happens a lot in the case of ongoing sexual abuse, and it can also happen with single-incident assaults. Your body is designed to respond to sexual stimulation in certain ways, and there is no reason to feel guilty for having a normal physical response. This type of reaction does not mean that you asked for the assault or wanted it to happen. Recognize the pleasure for what it was: a biological response to stimulation, and nothing else.

In your recovery, you will need compassion and understanding from others. But you will also, and perhaps most important, need those things from yourself. Focus on your recovery and on moving forward, rather than blaming yourself.

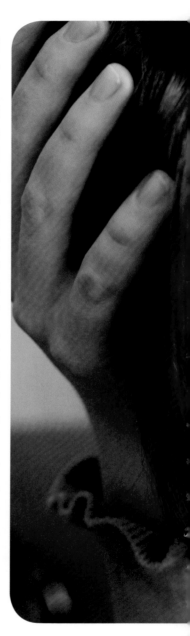

DEPRESSION

The trauma of sexual assault can sometimes cause you to fall into depression, to become so sad that it is

People who have been sexually assaulted often shut down their emotions and fall into depression. If you feel yourself detaching from your emotions, talk to someone and ask for help.

debilitating, or to shut down your emotions altogether. Depression is especially common for people who have experienced sexual assault or abuse during their childhood. Although everyone experiences sadness at some point in life, sadness becomes depression when it hangs on for a prolonged period of time and the symptoms begin to interfere with the person's daily life. Symptoms of depression include:

- Loss of appetite or excessive eating
- Inability to concentrate
- Uncontrollable negative thoughts
- Unusual irritability or aggressiveness
- Self-destructive behavior, such as excessive drinking or drug use
- Sleeping too much or too little
- Thoughts of suicide

If you experience five or more of these symptoms for more than two weeks, you may be clinically depressed, and you should seek the help of a professional counselor or therapist. And if you are having suicidal thoughts, don't wait. Talk to a counselor as soon as possible.

POST-TRAUMATIC STRESS DISORDER

Post-traumatic stress disorder (PTSD) develops out of normal coping mechanisms in an unbearably traumatic situation. People who have fought in wars experience

Rape Trauma Syndrome

Rape trauma syndrome (RTS) is very similar to PTSD. But while PTSD refers to reactions to any life-threatening situation, RTS refers to the unique effects of feeling like one's life is threatened during a rape or any other type of sexual violence. Like PTSD, this syndrome occurs when the normal immediate responses to a rape or sexual assault do not go away after a few weeks, but continue to disrupt the victim's life and halt recovery. RTS usually occurs in female victims, child victims, or adolescent victims. It is characterized by many of the same symptoms as PTSD, but it also includes disruption of the victim's sexual life and development. For child and adolescent victims, it can include nausea, vomiting, or bedwetting, which are normal childhood responses to stress. Adolescents often describe feelings of embarrassment, and they worry that they will not be able to relate normally to their peers or have a normal social life. Of course, those feelings are expected and do not always indicate RTS. But if they're hanging on, hindering recovery, and disrupting your daily life, they might be RTS. If you are experiencing any of these reactions and they are not subsiding over time, ask your therapist about rape trauma syndrome.

PTSD. So do people who have been abused, assaulted, or raped. After a trauma, it is normal to feel anxious or on edge, to feel detached, sad, or numb, and to have trouble putting the event out of one's mind. But if these symptoms hang on for a long time after the incident is over, it is possible that they have become PTSD. As with all the other effects discussed in this section, PTSD is definitely treatable with therapy. Here are signs that can give warning of the condition. Remember that all of these things are normal in the immediate aftermath of an assault, but if they persist for months or even for years following the actual incident, they may indicate PTSD:

- Recurring dreams or nightmares about the assault
- Flashbacks
- Intense physical reactions (such as sweating, nausea, or accelerated heart rate) to reminders of the assault
- Difficulty sleeping
- Feeling detached or numb
- Losing or blocking out memories related to the assault
- Feeling on edge all the time, jumping when you hear loud noises or sirens, etc.
- Physical aches and pains
- Feeling depressed, hopeless, or suicidal

SEXUAL ASSAULT AND BODY IMAGE

Being raped or sexually assaulted can have extremely adverse effects on your image of and relationship to your own body. Sexual assault survivors are especially vulnerable to eating disorders. Some people develop an eating

Sexual violence can have a negative effect on a survivor's body image, causing the survivor to be excessively critical or have an unrealistic view of his or her body.

disorder such as anorexia, in which they starve them-selves and/or exercise excessively as an attempt to exert control. By denying herself food, an assault survivor may feel that she is reclaiming control over her body. A similar thought process may occur in bulimia, the cycle of bing-ing on food and then purging through vomiting or the use of laxatives. Many survivors also deliberately gain weight in an attempt to make themselves unattractive, which they feel will prevent future assaults. All of these things are ultimately harmful to the body and the recovery process. Although the rationalizations behind them are completely understandable, it is important for your own safety that you avoid falling into these behaviors. If you feel like your relationship with food is becoming unhealthy, talk to a counselor right away. He or she can help you find health-ier ways to cope with your emotions.

In addition to contributing to eating disorders, being assaulted may give a person a skewed perception of his or her own body. Assault survivors often become overly critical of their bodies and experience a significant drop in self-esteem. They sometimes become unable to see their bodies realistically, or they feel detached from them altogether. Lots of abuse survivors report feeling as though their bodies don't belong to them. It also com-monly becomes difficult for survivors to be physically intimate with people after being assaulted. Many have a hard time feeling safe in sexual situations, or they feel so self-critical that they are afraid to let other people look at them intimately.

If you experience any of these feelings, know that they are a normal psychological response to the trauma that you've been through. But also do your best to work through them. A counselor can help. Writing in a journal can also help. There are all kinds of books out there that focus on body image and ways to build or rebuild your self-esteem and learn to be intimate in healthy ways. You can definitely develop a healthy relationship to your body and a healthy and realistic perception of yourself.

CHAPTER 4

Beginning to Heal

Self-care after a rape or assault begins with visiting the emergency room and seeking crisis counseling, but it definitely does not end there. It is an ongoing process, encompassing lots of different things. It includes the smallest, everyday personal care tasks, such as hygiene, nutrition, and sleep. It includes exercise and keeping up with any medications and other treatments prescribed by a doctor or mental health professional. It also includes taking care of oneself emotionally, doing the things that are necessary to feel happy and be mentally healthy. Concentrating on self-care can be healing and empowering, since it puts much of the responsibility for recovery in the survivor's own hands. But it can be difficult, in the wake of rape or sexual assault, to remember all the things you need to do to take care of yourself. Here are some suggestions for ways that

Setting Healthy Boundaries

For people who have been sexually assaulted—and for people who haven't, too—it can be confusing to determine sexual boundaries and decide what kind of sexual behavior they find personally acceptable. Everyone gets conflicting messages about sex. It seems as though everyone is talking about it, but no one agrees. From parents to religious organizations to the media to your friends, everyone has opinions about what you should and shouldn't do and what your sexual behavior means. All this chatter and all these differing opinions can make it hard to determine what you truly want. If you've been sexually assaulted, someone at some point took that choice away from you, and that can make things more confusing. When you find yourself in a consensual sexual situation, and you add hormones to the equation (we all have them!), your mind can get pretty fuzzy. It's important to think about where you stand and what you want before you are in the heat of the moment. Mentally prepare yourself for scenarios that might occur, and decide how you want to handle these situations before they actually happen. Journaling can be really helpful, as can talking with friends or adults whose advice you trust. Remember that your body is your own, and what you do with it is entirely up to you. You have the right and the responsibility to be assertive and definite about what you do and do not want sexually. What you want doesn't always stay the same; your feelings about sex may evolve or change depending on where you are in your life and your recovery, and that is perfectly OK. Just make sure that you take the time to think about your desires and boundaries. Remember that no one ever has the right to pressure you into things that you don't really want to do. No matter what is going on in your life sexually or romantically, make sure that you stay focused on your own physical and emotional wellness so that your decisions are coming from a healthy place.

PHYSICAL SELF-CARE

When you're healthy, things like hygiene, nutrition, and sleep usually come as second nature. But when you've experienced a trauma like sexual assault, the resulting anxiety and depression can make these things much more difficult than they used to be. This is why it is so important to be intentional about them in the wake of an assault.

Depression can cause you to stop caring about personal hygiene, such as showering regularly, changing your clothes, and brushing your teeth. When you feel hopeless about life in general, these things seem futile or unnecessary. But neglecting your hygiene only feeds your depression, making you feel more out of control. Make a point to shower regularly, brush your teeth, and wear clean clothes, even if you don't feel like doing those things. Keeping up with your hygiene is an important and necessary part of self-care.

Sexual abuse and assault, and the resulting depression, will often cause victims to neglect their nutrition. This neglect manifests itself differently for different people. Some victims may stop eating altogether, while others may overeat. There is a strong connection between eating disorders and sexual assault. Studies have found that 30 percent of women who suffer from bulimia are rape survivors. Some people deny themselves food to the point of becoming unhealthily thin, while others gain weight deliberately to make themselves unattractive. While doing these things may seem like exerting control over your

The connection between the mind and the body should never be underestimated. Physical activity can be essential in keeping your spirits up during your recovery.

own body, they are ultimately harmful. Instead of engaging in unhealthy behaviors, you can demonstrate control over your body in beneficial ways, like by exercising safely and eating nutritious (and delicious) food.

Sleep is incredibly important to one's physical and mental health. Victims of trauma often have trouble sleeping due to anxiety, fear, or depression. Lack of sleep can affect a person's health in lots of ways. It can dull concentration and affect judgment, contribute to obesity, and put people at risk for conditions such as diabetes and heart disease. If you are having trouble sleeping, try some natural methods first, like meditation, yoga, taking a warm bath, or doing anything else that helps you relax. If none of these things work, talk to your doctor, who may be able to prescribe medicine that can help you sleep. Getting enough sleep will improve your mood, make you more alert, and strengthen your judgment and perception, making other aspects of your recovery much easier.

EMOTIONAL SELF-CARE

Taking care of yourself emotionally is just as important as taking care of your physical needs. When you've gone through something as painful as a rape or any other type of sexual assault, it can be tempting to simply push it to the back of your mind and try to forget about it. But chances are, you will heal much more thoroughly and quickly if you process your emotions, rather than pushing them away. You can (and should) do this processing at

Never underestimate the importance of a good night's sleep. Getting adequate rest is necessary to keep your mind and body healthy during the recovery process.

your own pace and in your own way, but it is important that you do it somehow.

One way to process it is to talk with friends and family. Obviously, being sexually assaulted is not something that you'll want to discuss with just anyone, nor should you. But if you have a parent or another trusted adult, a sibling, or a friend with whom you feel comfortable discussing

Writing is a wonderful way to organize and express your thoughts, and it can be a very helpful outlet for processing your feelings about your rape or assault.

deeply personal things, it can help to share your feelings with that person. The anger and sadness that come from sexual assault are a very heavy burden to bear on your own. Just having someone else listen can help relieve some of that burden. Talking with someone else can also help you process your thoughts and verbalize them in ways you might not have thought of otherwise.

Keeping a journal is another thing that many people find helpful in recovering from any kind of trauma. There are a few reasons why journaling can be so healing. For one thing, it can function in a similar way to talking with other people; it helps you get some of the feelings off your chest and out of your head, making the burden a little lighter. For another thing, writing can help you organize your emotions into coherent thoughts, which makes them easier to process. Sometimes, in writing, you will discover thoughts and feelings that you didn't know were there. Having these thoughts written down means that you can come back to them later and deal with them, whether on your own or with someone else's help. Many survivors channel their feelings about their attacks into creative forms of writing, such as poems and stories.

Visual art is another way that people cope with emotions, either in addition to or instead of writing. Lots of people find activities such as painting, drawing, sculpting, or creating collages to be therapeutic. There is an entire field of counseling, called art therapy, devoted to this. That brings us to another part of recovery and self-care: deciding whether to enter counseling or therapy.

PROFESSIONAL CARE

The decision to seek counseling or psychotherapy is one that every person ultimately needs to make for himself or herself. Any type of therapy works better when the patient is invested in the work as much as the counselor or therapist is invested in it. Many people need time after an assault to process alone before they begin working with someone else. It can be frightening, at first, to confront the experience in the way that a therapist would require. Crisis counseling can definitely help a survivor in the immediate aftermath of a rape or sexual assault, but some survivors choose to stop there. You may be one of these people, or you may seek further counseling right away. But even if you don't immediately continue with therapy, it is never too late to seek someone else's help in dealing with your rape or assault. It is very important, no matter when you seek this help, to find the right therapist. You will need to find someone with whom you connect and someone who uses an approach that works for you. You

Seeking the guidance of a professional therapist is very important for recovery, whether you do it immediately following the attack or wait until months afterward.

may end up visiting several therapists before finding one who clicks for you, and that's OK.

If your family doesn't have the money to pay for therapy, there are still lots of options available to you. Lots of therapists charge for treatment using a sliding scale, meaning that people with lower incomes pay lower rates. Also, many rape crisis organizations can help survivors find ongoing treatment free of charge. Your family's economic status should not be a barrier to getting the help you need to recover. While it may, unfairly and unfortunately, make it a little more difficult, there are lots of people who are trying to change this, and whose job it is to help survivors obtain this care. Reach out to them.

10 Great Questions
to Ask Your Doctor or Nurse in the Emergency Room

 1 Will you give me medicine to prevent pregnancy?

 6 Are you legally obligated to report the rape to the police?

 2 Will you test me for sexually transmitted infections (STIs)?

 7 Can you make the 911 call for me if I'm too scared?

 3 Can you give me medicine to prevent STIs from taking hold?

 8 If I choose not to pursue legal action right now, will the hospital keep my rape kit on file?

 4 What are the possible side effects of the medicine?

 9 Where do I go for rape crisis counseling? Is someone available now?

 5 What is a rape kit?

 **10** What kind of follow-up medical treatment will I need?

CHAPTER 5

Activism and Support: Helping Others to Heal

Ine of the terrible things about rape and sexual assault is that they tend to leave survivors feeling as though their power has been taken away from them. In a previous section, we talked about eating disorders and other self-destructive activities that some victims engage in to try to regain a feeling of control and agency in their lives. This section discusses healthier ways that survivors can take back their power: helping others to heal and taking action to make the world safer and help prevent others from being victimized. In taking action and helping others, you help yourself move from being a victim to a survivor.

Talking with other assault survivors in a support group, whether it meets online or in person, can be a huge step in the healing process.

SUPPORT GROUPS AND ONLINE COMMUNITIES

Participating in in-person support groups or online support communities is one way that survivors can help others while also continuing their own healing process. Many support groups have weekly or monthly physical meetings to discuss trauma and recovery, and many communities exist online only. Both types of support groups have their advantages. For some, it helps to meet face-to-face and hear people's voices and see their facial expressions during a discussion. However, others are uncomfortable discussing their assaults in person, do not have the time or the transportation to attend an in-person meeting, or are simply shy around strangers. There are lots of online support communities that can be incredibly helpful for people who are not comfortable with in-person meetings.

For many sexual assault survivors, it is absolutely essential to connect with other people their own age that can identify with their situations. Community organizations may have peer support groups for teenagers recovering from sexual assault. If your local rape crisis organization does not have a group already set up for teenagers, it should be able to direct you to such a group somewhere else. Community centers for LGBTQ (lesbian, gay, bisexual, transgender, and questioning) individuals can also be very helpful with this, and they may have support groups for teenagers of all orientations who are recovering from assault.

EDUCATING YOURSELF AND OTHERS ABOUT SAFETY

Sexual assault is ALWAYS the fault of the attacker, not the victim. In many cases, there is nothing the victim could have done to prevent the assault. Even if the

Self-defense classes can help you to feel empowered and give you tools to fight off attackers, as well as giving you the mental and physical benefits of fitness.

victim was assaulted while intoxicated, while walking alone at night, or while in any type of precarious situation, that absolutely does not mean that he or she "asked for it" or that the attacker had any right to assault the victim. Regardless of the circumstances, every person has the right to consent to or refuse sexual activity. If someone takes that right away from you, that person has committed a serious violation. That being said, there are some things you can do to protect yourself. Have a plan of action if you find yourself in a dangerous situation, sexual or otherwise. This doesn't guarantee that nothing bad will ever happen to you, but it can help you be prepared if something does.

One thing you can do is seek out self-defense training. Many organizations offer this training at little or no cost. It can be very beneficial to have physical tricks in your back pocket in case you are ever in an assault situation. Of course, being prepared to physically fight off an attacker will not always prevent a sexual assault from happening, but it will make you feel less helpless if that situation arises. Check with community centers in your area, or ask a rape crisis counselor about self-defense training. Martial arts classes may be helpful in this regard, too.

It is wise to have a friend accompany you if you are walking home after dark, especially if you are intoxicated or if your judgment is otherwise compromised. Lots of college campuses offer a service where you can call and ask for a partner, and it will send someone to walk you home. If you don't have anyone to walk with you, at least call someone and keep him or her on the phone while

How Your Parents Can Help You

One of the most difficult parts of coping with sexual assault can be talking with your parents about it. It is always hard to talk with your parents about sex, and it's even harder to talk with them about such a sensitive subject as being sexually assaulted. Your parents may need to seek therapy themselves to cope with what has happened to you, especially if your attacker was a family member, a family friend, or someone else that your parents trusted. If your parents do enter therapy, it is important that their therapy process be separate from yours. It is usually a good idea for parents and children to have completely separate therapists for their individual sessions. Family therapy can be helpful, but it should be in addition to individual therapy. Often, people who have been assaulted find that they have lost faith in their parents' ability to protect them. This is especially true if the assault has been ongoing and the abuser is someone that the victim's parents trusted. If you feel that your parents didn't stop what was happening and didn't prevent it, it can become difficult to talk with them about the abuse or assault. Having a third party there to mediate can be very effective in building or rebuilding trust between children and parents. But again, family therapy should be separate from individual therapy. One of the great things about talking with a therapist is that he or she is there to listen to and help you, and he or she has your best interests, and only your best interests, at heart. This is why it is so important for family members to have separate therapists, even if they also go to therapy together.

you are making your way home. Again, this doesn't guar-antee safety, but if someone else knows where you are and is aware of your movements, it may deter potential attackers. It will also increase the possibility of getting help if someone does attack you. If you drop your phone or suddenly stop talking, the person on the other end will know that something is wrong, and he or she will be able to call 911.

In addition to taking these steps to preserve your safety, encourage others to do the same. If you notice that a friend is drunk and putting himself or herself in a precarious situation, have your friend's back and step in. If a friend has to walk home at night, offer to drive her or walk with her. Do what you can to help your friends be mindful of their own safety.

OPPORTUNITIES FOR ACTIVISM

There are lots of ways to network with other people who are concerned about creating a safe society and protect-ing people from sexual assault. Many organizations exist to help these people meet each other and work together. These organizations have lots of different opportunities for getting involved and volunteering.

Most rape crisis organizations operate help lines that offer emergency support and crisis intervention. Consider volunteering for these help lines. When you are a survivor yourself, you have empathy and a shared perspective that someone who has not been assaulted doesn't have.

Taking part in activism, including marches and rallies to protest sexual violence, can help you meet other survivors and feel as though you are taking back some control.

Since you've been through the trauma yourself, you can help guide others through the reporting process and point them toward resources that have been helpful to you in your recovery.

Lots of organizations put on marches and rallies to protest sexual violence and demand safe streets and a safer society for women and for all people. Definitely

By helping and supporting each other, survivors of rape and sexual assault can move through the healing process and gain back control of their lives and their emotions.

consider attending these marches and rallies. It can be exhilarating, uplifting, and empowering to be around a huge crowd of people who are all taking a stand for the same thing. Also, attending these events can be a great way to meet other people who have been through the same kind of trauma and who can become a support system for you.

Your assault is something that will always be a part of your life and your history. As much as you may want to simply erase the memory, it will always be with you. If you don't confront it honestly and move through a recovery process, it will surface in other, more destructive ways. But of course, you don't want to spend your whole life feeling like a victim. That is why it is so important to build relationships with other people who understand what you've been through and to help others through their own recovery process. In building these relationships and doing something proactive, you will become a survivor and not a victim, and you will come to see yourself as part of a community of survivors. In this way, you can take back the power that you lost during the assault and join with other people who are trying to create a safer world, where fewer and fewer people are hurt by sexual violence.

ADVOCATE Someone who speaks for another person and helps protect his or her rights, especially during legal proceedings. Many rape crisis organizations have volunteers who will provide this service at the hospital, during the reporting process, and during further legal action.

BODY IMAGE One's own perception of one's body and feelings about it. Sexual assault survivors often struggle with maintaining a healthy body image.

CHILD SEXUAL ABUSE Anytime an adult, be it a family member, a family friend, a teacher, or anyone else, has sexual contact with a minor, regardless of whether it is consensual or not.

CRISIS COUNSELING Counseling that a rape or assault survivor receives in the immediate aftermath of the assault, often at the hospital after the medical examination has taken place.

FAMILY THERAPY Therapy that helps parents and children learn to talk together and rebuild trust. It should always be done separately from and in addition to individual therapy for the survivor.

GROPING Unwanted touch of a sexual nature. Groping is a form of sexual assault.

HELP LINE A service offered by many rape crisis organizations in which a victim can call a toll-free number to receive crisis counseling and be directed to local resources that can help in reporting and recovery.

INCESTUOUS RAPE Rape committed by a family member.

POST-TRAUMATIC STRESS DISORDER (PTSD) A syndrome that occurs when normal physical and psychological responses to a life-threatening situation do not go away when the danger is removed but hang on and affect the survivor's everyday functioning.

RAPE Sexual assault that includes penetration of the anus or vagina with the penis, fingers, or a foreign object.

RAPE KIT The tools used to collect evidence in the emergency room after a rape. The evidence is kept on file to be potentially used in prosecution of the attacker.

RAPE TRAUMA SYNDROME (RTS) A syndrome similar to PTSD but is also characterized by responses to a life-threatening sexual situation, such as long-term difficulty with sexual functioning and feelings of shame or embarrassment.

RECOVERY The process of dealing with being raped or sexually assaulted; the act of trying to return to a state of physical and emotional health and normalcy.

REPORTING Telling the police about a rape, sexual assault, or any other crime.

SELF-BLAME A common occurrence in which assault survivors experience unwarranted feelings of guilt and begin to blame themselves for their attacks.

SELF-CARE All of the things that a person can do on his or her own to stay physically and emotionally healthy, such as good hygiene, routine exercise, and sleeping regularly.

SELF-DEFENSE Physical techniques that an individual can learn that may be helpful in fighting off potential attackers.

SEXUAL ASSAULT An attack of a sexual nature, using physical force.

SEXUAL HARASSMENT Lewd comments, indecent exposure, dirty jokes, and other unwanted or coercive (but non-physical) sexual behavior.

SUPPORT GROUP A group of people who gather intentionally, whether in person or online, to talk about their shared traumas and help each other through the recovery process.

FOR MORE INFORMATION

BC Society for Male Survivors of Sexual Abuse
#202 - 1252 Burrard Street
Vancouver, BC V6Z 1Z1
Canada
(604) 682-6482
Web site: http://www.bc-malesurvivors.com
This Canadian organization provides treatment, support,
    and advocacy specifically for male survivors of sexual
    assault and abuse.

GirlTHRIVE
30 Willow Street
Brooklyn, NY 11201
Web site: http://www.girlthrive.com
GirlTHRIVE provides advice about seeking help after
    sexual assault and other resources for survivors.
    The Web site includes a section where survivors can
    share their stories and read the stories of others.

MaleSurvivor
PMB 103
5505 Connecticut Ave NW
Washington, DC 20015-4181
Web site: http://www.malesurvivor.org
Started in 1988, this organization sponsors conferences
    and recovery weekends, provides an online support
    network, and directs male survivors to recovery
    resources, including therapy.

Pandora's Project
3109 West 50th Street, Suite #320
Minneapolis, MN 55410-2102
Web site: http://www.pandorasproject.org
Pandora's Project provides resources for survivors,
    including specialized sections for kids, teens, and
    male and LGBTQ survivors. It maintains an online
    support community, as well as a lending library for
    members of that community.

RAINN (Rape, Abuse, and Incest National Network)
2000 L Street NW, Suite 406
Washington, DC 20036
(202) 544-1034
National Sexual Assault Hotline: (800) 656-HOPE (4673)
Web site: http://www.rainn.org
Founded in 1995 by singer Tori Amos (herself a sexual
    assault survivor), RAINN is the largest U.S. organiza-
    tion fighting sexual assault. In addition to operating
    the twenty-four-hour National Sexual Assault Hotline
    (which connects survivors immediately with local
    rape crisis centers), it partners with local and national
    organizations and businesses to provide resources
    for recovery, education, and activism.

Sexual Assault Services Organization (SASO)
P.O. Box 2723
Durango, CO 81302

(970) 247-5400

Web site: http://www.durangosaso.org

SASO provides services for survivors, including recovery support and legal and medical advocacy, and it
engages in education and outreach.

Victoria Women's Sexual Assault Centre (VWSAC)

#511 - 620 View Street

Victoria, BC V8W 1J6

Canada

(250) 383-3232

Web site: http://www.vwsac.com

Located in Victoria, British Columbia, the VWSAC works
to "support, empower and advocate for" women who
have survived sexual violence.

WEB SITES

Due to the changing nature of Internet links, Rosen
Publishing has developed an online list of Web sites
related to the subject of this book. This site is updated
regularly. Please use this link to access the list:

http://www.rosenlinks.com/HELP/RASA

FOR FURTHER READING

Atkinson, Matt. *Letters to Survivors: Words of Comfort for Women Recovering from Rape*. Oklahoma City, OK: R.A.R. Publishing, 2010.

Bromley, Nicole Braddock. *Hush: Moving from Silence to Healing After Childhood Sexual Abuse*. Chicago, IL: Moody Publishers, 2007.

Daugherty, Dr. Lynn. *Why Me?: Help for Victims of Childhood Sexual Abuse*. Roswell, NM: Cleanan Press, 2007.

Friedman, Jaclyn. *What You Really Want: The Smart Girl's Shame-Free Guide to Sex and Safety*. Berkeley, CA: Seal Press, 2011.

Friedman, Jaclyn, and Jessica Valenti. *Yes Means Yes!: Visions of Female Sexual Power and a World Without Rape*. Berkeley, CA: Seal Press, 2008.

Maltz, Wendy. *The Sexual Healing Journey: A Guide for Survivors of Sexual Abuse*. New York, NY: William Morrow, 2012.

Matsakis, Aphrodite. *The Rape Recovery Handbook: Step-by-Step Help for Survivors of Sexual Assault*. Oakland, CA: New Harbinger, 2003.

Milligan, Greg Tyler. *A Beautiful World: One Son's Escape from the Snares of Abuse and Devotion*. Indianapolis, IN: Dog Ear Publishing, 2009.

Phelps, Shirley Itim Melo. *We Women of Many Shades and Hues: Daily Common Ground for Survivors of Childhood Sexual Abuse, Incest and Rape*. Los Gatos, CA: Robertson Publishing, 2008.

Robinson, Lori S. *I Will Survive: The African-American Guide to Healing from Sexual Assault and Abuse*. Berkeley, CA: Seal Press, 2003.

Sebold, Alice. *Lucky: A Memoir*. New York, NY: Scribner, 2002.

Smith, Charlene. *Whispers on My Skin: A Rape Survivor's Guide to Relearning Intimate Touch*. Cambridge, MA: Sunset Road, 2012.

After Silence. "Rape Trauma Syndrome." Retrieved August 19, 2012 (http://www.aftersilence.org/rape-trauma-syndrome.php).

American Academy of Child and Adolescent Psychiatry. "Facts for Families: Child Sexual Abuse." Retrieved August 16, 2012 (http://aacap.org/page.ww?name=Child+Sexual+Abuse&section=Facts+for+Families).

American Academy of Experts in Traumatic Stress. "What to Do If You're Raped." Retrieved August 16, 2012 (http://www.aaets.org/article118.htm).

Center for Women and Children in Crisis. "What to Do After Experiencing Sexual Assault." Retrieved September 14, 2012 (http://cwcic.org/cwcic_after_assault.php).

Centers for Disease Control and Prevention. "Sexual Violence: Facts at a Glance." Retrieved August 16, 2012 (http://www.cdc.gov/ViolencePrevention/pdf/SV-DataSheet-a.pdf).

Columbia University. "Eating Disorders and Sexual Assault." Retrieved August 16, 2012 (http://health.columbia.edu/topics/eating-disorders/sexual-assault).

Harvard Medical School Division of Sleep Medicine. "Consequences of Insufficient Sleep." Retrieved August 16, 2012 (http://healthysleep.med.harvard.edu/healthy/matters/consequences).

HelpGuide.org. "Post-Traumatic Stress Disorder: Symptoms, Treatment and Self-Help." Retrieved August 16, 2012 (http://www.helpguide.org/mental/post_traumatic_stress_disorder_symptoms_treatment.htm).

HelpGuide.org. "Understanding Depression: Signs, Symptoms, Causes and Help." Retrieved August 16, 2012 (http://www.helpguide.org/mental/depression _signs_types_diagnosis_treatment.htm).

Menard, Kim S. *Reporting Rape: A Social Ecology Perspective*. New York, NY: LFB Scholarly Publishing, 2005.

National Center for Victims of Crime. "Reporting on Child Sexual Abuse." Retrieved August 10, 2012 (http:// www.victimsofcrime.org/help-for-crime-victims).

Rape, Abuse, and Incest National Network. "Reporting Rape." Retrieved August 10, 2012 (http://www.rainn .org/get-information/legal-information/reporting-rape).

Women's Sexual Assault Centre. "The Impact of Sexual Violence." Retrieved August 16, 2012 (http://www .vwsac.com/impact-of-sv.html).

INDEX

 A

acquaintance rape, 16
activism, 56, 62–65
anorexia, 42
art therapy, 51

 B

body image, and rape/sexual
    assault, 40–43
boundaries, setting healthy
    sexual, 45
bulimia, 42, 46

 C

child sexual abuse, 12–13, 16,
    38, 39
crisis centers, contacting, 29,
    44, 52, 58, 62

D

date rape, 16
depression, 36–38, 46
    symptoms of, 38

 E

eating disorders, 40–42, 46, 56
emergency room, visiting after
    rape, 5, 20–22, 44
    questions to ask, 55

 G

groping, 11

 H

healing, 44–54

 I

incestuous rape, 16

 J

journal, keeping a, 43, 51

L

legal attention, seeking, 19–20,
    26–29

ABOUT THE AUTHOR

Rebecca Klein writes books for young adults. She is currently working on a master's degree in English education. She grew up in Detroit and lives in Brooklyn.

PHOTO CREDITS

Cover © iStockphoto.com/Todor Tcetkov; pp. 5, 15 Comstock/ Thinkstock; p. 8 Photodisc/Thinkstock; p. 10 Ghislain & Marie David de Lossy/The Image Bank/Getty Images; p. 13 © iStockphoto.com/ Chris Schmidt; p. 19 Sara Press/Workbook Stock/Getty Images; p. 21 Nicole Waring/the Agency Collection/Getty Images; pp. 23, 34–35 © Phanie/SuperStock; p. 25 Photo Researchers/Getty Images; p. 32 Xavier Arnau/E+/Getty Images; pp. 36–37 LeoGrand /E+/Getty Images; p. 41 iStockphoto/Thinkstock; p. 47 BananaStock /Thinkstock; p. 49 Brand New Images/Stone/Getty Images; p. 50 Ryan McVay/Photodisc/Thinkstock; pp. 52–53 © Dana White/ PhotoEdit; p. 57 © iStockphoto.com/Jeanell Norvell; pp. 58–59 Chris Schmidt/Vetta/Getty Images; p. 63 Spencer Platt/Getty Images; pp. 64–65 Jupiterimages/Brand X Pictures/Thinkstock; background pattern (telephones) pp. 1, 7, 9, 18, 27, 30, 39, 44, 45, 56, 61 © iStockphoto.com/Oksana Pasishnychenko; cover and interior telephone icons © iStockphoto.com/miniature.

Except for pages 52–53 and 63, individuals pictured are models and are used for illustrative purposes only.

Designer: Nicole Russo; Editor: Bethany Bryan;
Photo Researcher: Karen Huang